The Water Cycle

by Anne Minor

Scott Foresman
is an imprint of

Glenview, Illinois • Boston, Massachusetts • Mesa, Arizona
Shoreview, Minnesota • Upper Saddle River, New Jersey

llustrator 4 Dan Trush

Photographs
Every effort has been made to secure permission and provide appropriate credit for photographic material. The publisher deeply regrets any omission and pledges to correct errors called to its attention in subsequent editions.

Unless otherwise acknowledged, all photographs are the property of Pearson Education, Inc.

Photo locators denoted as follows: Top (T), Center (C), Bottom (B), Left (L), Right (R), Background (Bkgd)

CVR David Wall/Danita Delimont Agency/Digital Railroad; **1** © Will Stanton/Alamy Images; **3** (B) © Robert Destefano/Alamy, (L) © Will Stanton/Alamy Images, (T) © Klaus Hackenberg/zefa/Corbis; **5** ©JupiterImages/Thinkstock/Alamy; **6** Guy Llorca/Jupiter Images; **7** © ImageState/Alamy Images; **8** David Wall/Danita Delimont Agency/Digital Railroad; **9** image100/Jupiter Images; **10** © Randy Faris/Corbis; **11** © AGB Photo/Alamy; **12** © Douglas Menuez/Getty Images.

ISBN 13: 978-0-328-39440-1
ISBN 10: 0-328-39440-8

1 2 3 4 5 6 7 8 9 10 V0G1 17 16 15 14 13 12 11 10 09 08

Water is everywhere. We drink it every day. We could not live without it. Ice is water too. Even the air is full of water. Air contains an invisible gas called water vapor. Ice, liquid, and water vapor are the three forms that water can take.

Water vapor

Liquid water

Ice

Water is always on the move. It moves from the oceans to the sky. Then it falls to the ground as rain or snow. Finally, it flows back to the oceans, and the process starts again. This happens over and over. That is why it is called the water cycle.

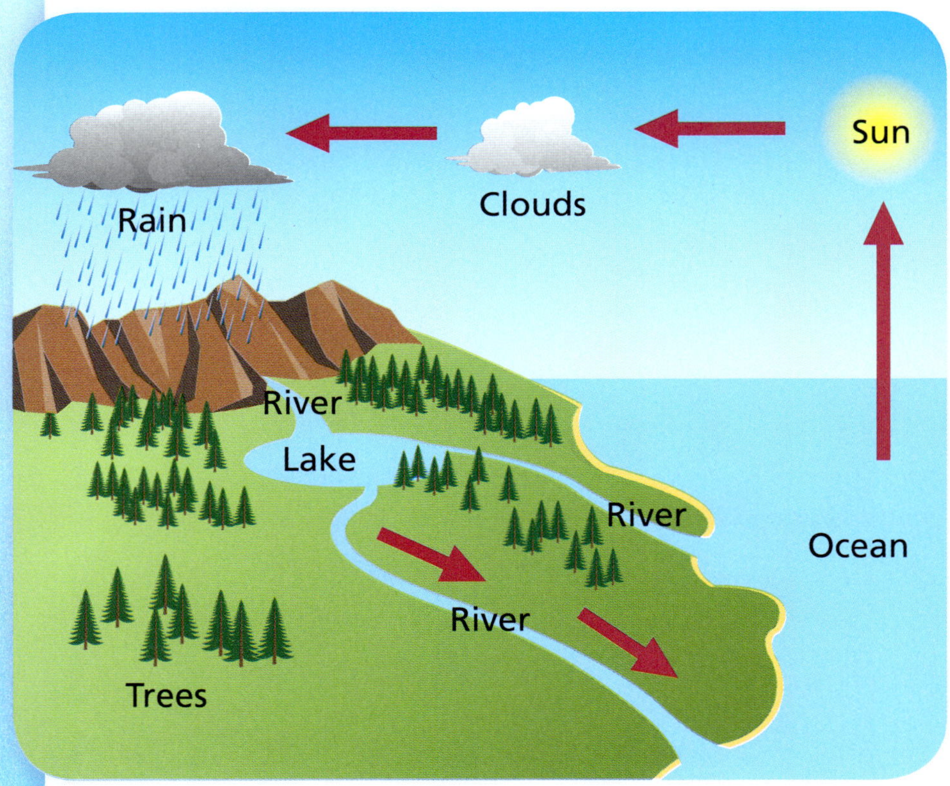

The oceans play a big part in the water cycle. The sun heats the oceans' water. That heat makes the liquid water change into water vapor. The water vapor then rises into the air.

The sun and the oceans are part of the water cycle.

The water vapor rises higher and higher above the Earth. As the air gets colder, the water vapor changes into tiny droplets of liquid water. We say that the water vapor *condenses* into liquid water. These tiny droplets float and make clouds. When the air is cold enough, the water droplets freeze into ice.

Clouds are made of tiny droplets of floating water or ice.

When bits of ice join together, they become heavy and start to fall. This water falls to the ground as rain or, when it is colder, as snow or sleet. Some of this water ends up in rivers.

Rain falls from clouds.

Rivers carry Earth's water back to the oceans. Rivers pick up some salt and other minerals as they flow over land. The salt dissolves in the water.

Water moving in rivers is part of the water cycle.

The water from rivers flows into the oceans. The salt from the rivers goes into the oceans too. This is one way that the oceans get salt. We can't drink salt water—we need fresh water to drink.

When water rises as vapor from oceans to the air, the salt is left behind. The water that falls back to Earth as rain or snow becomes fresh.

The water finally makes it back to the oceans.

Only a small part of all the water on Earth is fresh. There are more people living on Earth today than ever before. That means that more people are using Earth's fresh water supply. That's why it's important to conserve, or save, fresh water. Two easy ways to help conserve water are to turn off the water while you brush your teeth and to take shorter showers.

We can all help conserve water.

Fresh water is an important substance. We cannot live without it. But it is more than just a refreshing drink. Fresh water also helps our bodies digest food. It helps plants grow. It keeps all living things alive.

Everyone needs water.

Water goes around and around in a cycle. The oceans are part of the cycle. Rain and rivers are part of the cycle too. The water cycle keeps our water fresh and clean. We'd all be thirsty without water. We cannot live without water!

Natural wetlands help the Earth's water cycle.